the

LAUNCH BOOK

The Little Guide to Launching Your Book

Les Zigomanis

First published by Busybird Publishing 2015
Copyright © 2015 Les Zigomanis

ISBN 978-0-9925226-0-5

Cover image by Blaise van Hecke
Cover design by Busybird Publishing
Layout and typesetting: Les Zigomanis
Illustrations: Kev Howlett
Proofreaders: Terri Giuretis, Erin Dite, Courtney
Baxter, Rebecca Courtney, Klara Cole, Shevon Higgins

Busybird Publishing
PO Box 855
Eltham Victoria
Australia 3095

www.busybird.com.au

Contents

Foreword   i
In Support of Celebration:
The Importance of Book Launches   i

The launch   1
So what exactly is a book launch?   1
Why have a launch?   2

Choosing a date   5
When should you have your launch?   5
Will your book be ready?   5
Factoring other variables into the date   7
What is the best day and time
for a launch?   8

Budget   9

Venues   11
Is there a perfect venue?   14

Launch emcee   17

Getting a Launcher   19
   What is a launcher?   19
   Who is suitable?   20
   What to look out for   20

Sending out invitations   23
   What form your invitations will take   24
   Where to send your invitations   26
   Some other alternatives   27

Promoting   29

Catering   33
   Food   34
   Alcohol   34
   Other drinks   35

Staff for your launch   37
   Drinks   37
   The book table   38

Additional needs for the launch   41
   A podium   41
   A microphone   41
   Promotional paraphernalia   41
   Decorations   42
   Float   42
   Eftpos   42
   A speech   43
   An extract from your book   43

Tips for public presenting   45

Rehearse   45

Hold something heavy in your hands   45

Alcohol and presentation   46

Stand behind your podium   46

Setting up your launch   47

A focus centre   47

Chairs   48

A book table   48

A food and drinks table   50

What happens at the launch   51

The book table   55

What happens at the book table?   55

Recapping   57

It's a wrap!   61

Foreword

In support of celebration:
The importance of book launches

Celebrating the release of a book is important. It is somewhere in the middle of the 'process'.

I often think of this ceremony as the champagne bottle hitting the bow of the boat. It completes the creative process, and it marks the beginning of another journey.

This is the public passage where you, as the author, have little control. A launch allows your work that first safe voyage across the rough seas of general public opinion before you are at the mercy of reviewers, of bookshop owners and of the shallow tide of marketing.

This commemoration should be an opportunity for you, as the writer, to say thank you to all those who helped along the way, a means of thanking your friends and family.

It is also an opportunity for you to sell your book. It is your greatest chance to sell many copies.

Your friends and family, and their friends and family (people you may not know) will be so pleased for you and so relieved the creative process is done with, that they will buy your book.

It's the generosity of humanity working well. There is hope and joy at these events.

This seems to happen only at launches.

Get in quickly.

Don't waste time.

Once your book is bound, organise the launch.

My tips:

+ Invite every person you have ever met.

+ Be kind to every person who talks to you about your book.

+ Enjoy the champers.

Bon voyage.

Christine Gordon
– *Events Manager*
Readings.

The launch

So what exactly is a book launch?
Is it like a rocket launch, where your book is launched into outer space?

Well, not quite.

Consider the launch the birth of your book, when it comes out into the world and everybody celebrates its arrival.

Whether you've self-published or been published by a huge commercial publisher, your book will need a launch, and more often than not, that's going to be left to you!

Why have a launch?
You'd be forgiven for thinking that once you've written and published your book, your work is done.

It's not.

You then need to promote your book every chance you get. Think about interviews you could pursue, on radio or in the local paper. Consider places you could submit your book for review. Or libraries and/or bookstores where you might give talks about your book. There are lots of opportunities for exposure and promotion.

And it all begins with your launch. This is where you let everybody know your book exists. This is where you get the momentum rolling.

So let's begin.

Choosing a date

The first thing you have to work out is *when* your launch will be. This is not as straightforward a decision as it seems. There are some factors to consider.

When should you have your launch?

Set a date and start planning. Invitations should go out 4–5 weeks beforehand. This will give you time to generate interest in your launch, to send out invitations, and to advertise (all to be covered later).

Will your book be ready?

Some authors schedule their launch days after their book's due back from the printers, believing everything will just fall into place. Hmmm. This is great if you have a reliable printer, such as MacPherson's, and you know your book will be ready exactly on the date you've been told.

But we need to allow for mishaps. Printers have delays or make errors. Longer lead times may be required. If printed overseas, your book might get stuck in Customs.

Give yourself at least a week's leeway from the time your book's printed to the launch date, just in case there are unforeseen delays.

There's nothing worse, after all, than having a birthday without the guest of honour.

Factoring other variables into the date

Just as we need to make sure our book will be ready for the launch, there are a couple of other things we need to make sure will also be available for our chosen date.

These are:

+ **Our venue**: venues might have other functions on your chosen day. Be flexible. Have contingency dates planned. Or contingency venues!

+ **Your launcher's availability**: your launcher will be discussed in greater detail shortly, but be sure they're also available on the date you'd like to have your launch. If they're not and you're fixed on a date, then make sure you have alternatives for launchers.

What is the best day and time for a launch?

There is no definitive time. It's up to you. Just keep in mind there are benefits and drawbacks to whatever day and time you choose. A weekend might be great as it'll allow people to bring kids, but it might conflict with sporting events or other functions, which'll draw away possible guests.

Weekday evenings may be more open for some, but you have to remember that people work and might be too tired to venture out afterward, and if they have young kids who have school next day, they might prefer not to be out on a weeknight. A weeknight in winter might be particularly uninviting.

Consider what the best time is for you and your book. If you've written a children's or young adult book, you might want a time suitable for people to bring kids. If you've written a steamy, erotic thriller, an evening might be more appropriate.

Budget

It's important to determine how much you have to spend for your launch.

It'd be great if you had the luxury to rent a large hall, get embossed invitations, fully cater the function, etc., but the reality is that you're probably operating frugally, particularly if you've self-published.

Not to fear! You don't have to sell a kidney to have the launch you want.

Just keep in mind your budget as you start putting things together.

One idea might be to use a diary or spreadsheet to keep track of your budget and expenses.

Venues

You can have a launch anywhere –
in a house, in a park, in a hall, or on
the moon.

You are limited only by your
imagination.

But there are practicalities to consider:

+ Cost

+ Where your guests will be comfortable

+ Available toilets

+ Available parking

+ Weather (if you're considering outdoors)

+ Insurance

+ Accessibility.

You might find somewhere that doesn't perfectly accommodate one (or more) of these features, e.g. the only toilet might be in the shopping arcade next door, or the only public parking might be down the street.

Remember, some people will decide

whether they're going to come contingent on the location and the facilities available.

Is there a perfect venue?

No. There's only a venue perfect for you.

You might want to consider somewhere related to books in order to maintain that theme related to publishing, launches, and the literary community. Or you might consider something related to your book.

If your budget is thin and you can't afford the local town hall, here are some great alternatives:

+ **A library**: libraries will usually be free and can have sections set aside for functions. Some also have function or community rooms which are cheap and give you privacy and seclusion from the rest of the library.

+ **A bookstore**: like libraries, some bookstores have function areas that can be hired out. Unlike libraries, they can be expensive. But if your book is going to be stocked by the bookstore in question, you might be able to negotiate a deal which is suitable for both of you.

+ **Scout halls, etc.**: these are also cheap, and usually provide chairs and tables which you can set-up.

+ **Local councils** often have rooms available for hire.

Contact the administrators of any of these venues to discuss availability and cost.

You could even have the launch in your own home, although if your launch is open to the public, this means you'll be throwing open your doors to strangers. Insurance can also become an issue.

Launch emcee

The launch emcee will host proceedings, introduce the launcher, and perhaps even introduce you.

The emcee is a luxury. If you have a friend who can perform these duties, that is great. But if your budget is limited and your resources few, this is a duty you can undertake yourself.

Getting a launcher

What is a launcher?

In simplest terms, a launcher is somebody with either celebrity or relevance (or both) who'll go up, charm the audience, talk a little about you, your book, and perhaps even read an extract from your book.

Once all this is done, they'll declare that your book is launched.

Who is suitable?

Anybody can launch a book. It's a case of finding somebody suitable for you.

Some might like a celebrity, which could help promotionally.

Others might consider somebody who has some connection to the subject matter of their book – if you've written a cookbook, for instance, an accomplished chef might be ideal. If you could afford it, you could get a celebrity chef.

Anybody can launch a book. It's just a case of finding the best fit for your needs.

What to look out for

Just be aware that if you do pursue a celebrity launcher, they'll probably expect to be compensated for their time. So when you ask around, don't expect them to do it for free. Ask what they charge.

If your launcher is launching your book for free (lucky you!), you might consider rewarding them with a gift, e.g. flowers, chocolates, or a fruit basket.

Sending out invitations

Now that you have a venue and launcher booked, it's time to send out invitations.

The invitations will contain the following information:

+ Name of your book

+ Date and time of the launch

+ Location of the launch

+ Who'll be launching your book

+ Maybe an image of the book (cover)

+ An RSVP.

If the launcher is somebody of note, they can be a selling point.

You might also include a little snippet of what the book's about.

Finally, it's wise to include an RSVP as it'll give you some indication of the numbers you might expect. This can help with catering.

What form your invitations will take
Even if you have no design skills or any ability with a graphic program such as Photoshop, you can put together a simple but elegant document with all the necessary particulars.

Remember, the priority here isn't fanciness that doesn't tell people anything, but the details they require to sum-up whether your book will interest them, and thus where to go for the launch.

For example:

Please join us
as award-winning author,
Bob Smith,
launches the young adult novel:

The Dog That Could
by Rex Rover.

A stunning tale about a dog's
indomitable spirit and his
unswerving loyalty to a little boy.

Where: Busybird Publishing
2/118 Para Road
Montmorency, Victoria 3084
When: Sunday 25th July,
2.30pm.

Please RSVP by emailing
me@email.com

You could even dress up something like this by printing it on graphic stationery, or by writing it over the various stationery backgrounds which usually come with word processors (such as *Word*) or some mailboxes.

Where to send your invitations

If you have designed an invitation, save it as an image, like a .jpg. Many mailboxes allow you to insert images into the body of an email, which will preserve all the elements of your design.

Then send away!

A word of caution: some ISP servers prohibit you from sending emails en masse, as it gets flagged by their spam filters. The best method around this is to break down how many people you send it to at one time, e.g. send it to blocks of thirty people.

Some other alternatives

We live in an electronic age and social media has become prevalent in our lives. It allows us to connect to people instantaneously. Even if you are opposed to social media, as a tool it's not to be disregarded.

Facebook actually allows us to create an EVENT, which is a Facebook invitation to all your friends. If you make the invitation PUBLIC, it means that anybody on Facebook will be capable of seeing it also.

You will have to check Facebook HELP (or just use Google) to find the current way of creating an event (as Facebook is always changing), but they are easy and just a matter of providing answers for the prompts.

At the very least, you could invite everybody through a STATUS UPDATE, or do the same with a tweet on Twitter.

Other forms of social media (e.g. LinkedIn, Google+, etc.) will provide similar avenues, or at the least allow us to regularly spruik our launch.

Promoting

There is a whole world out there accessible at the click of a mouse.

This world includes such staples as:

- Facebook

- Twitter

- LinkedIn

- Google+

- Tumblr

- Email.

There's also a good chance that as time goes on, there'll be even more online alternatives and other social media platforms.

Also consider newsletters related to writing. There are a lot of organisations and groups that send out weekly or monthly e-newsletters.

Every state has a writing centre, which sends out media such as magazines and/or newsletters. Most times, they will be free. But, again, check costs. *Don't* assume. Also, keep in mind that to appear in a monthly magazine, you will have to book a number of weeks in advance.

If you've written a book about a certain topic – e.g. a book about dogs – see if there are any doggy newsletters or vet clinics that you can advertise in and which might have a readership interested in your book.

Write a media release and send it to your local newspaper. Try to find a good hook. Local newspapers like to promote stories about local writers and projects.

Lastly, you may want to condense your invitation into a flyer. These can be left (with permission) at libraries or bookstores (or, again, anywhere relevant to your book), or posted on noticeboards at schools, which teach writing and encourage their students to attend launches and other literary functions.

Catering

So what should you provide for the masses who will attend your launch?

Again, it's a matter of budget. But offering a little something is simple courtesy and should satisfy your guests so their focus remains on your launch and not on their grumbling stomachs.

Food

At the very least, providing a variety of finger-food gives guests something to nibble on. Stores like Safeway sell cheese platters that are inexpensive but offer a lot of variety. Other stores offer sandwich platters. This is where RSVPs help you gauge possible numbers and the requirements you'll have to fill.

Alcohol

Consider who your guests are going to be before you provide alcohol. The last thing you want are rowdy guests fuelled by booze who won't show your launch – or you – the courtesy you deserve. For this reason, you might want to limit the quantity and range of alcohol.

Alternatively, you might have your launch at a venue with a bar where patrons can buy their own drinks. You might want to turn it into a party. Just keep in mind the way the environment will unfold and what suits your launch.

Wine is something elegant and which is usually drunk in moderation.

You can also offer stubbies of beer, or pour into plastic glasses directly from the bottle.

Other drinks

Make sure you provide several non-alcoholic beverages for guests who don't drink.

Staff for your launch

Staff certainly makes it seem as if your launch is becoming officious and worldly and whilst you could survive without them, there are several areas you could do with help.

Don't panic, though. You needn't hit the employment agencies and fret about the cost of hiring professional staff.

Consider family members and/or friends as the cheapest (if not a free) avenue for staff.

Drinks

Will you have a table or bar for alcohol? In that case, you might want a bartender. A bartender will also help you ensure that alcohol won't be abused.

At some launches, people have the staff walking amongst the guests and offering refills.

The book table

You'll have a table at your launch dedicated just to your book – a display table. If you're not holding your launch at a bookstore, then – in all likelihood – you'll also be selling your book from this table.

And don't scoff. You will sell books!

Whilst you could see to this yourself, it'd be great if somebody else could handle the finances and monitor how many books are being sold.

After all, you'll be busy chatting with guests and regaling them with tales of your brilliance. So it's best if somebody else can handle the mundane work.

Just make sure whoever you choose for this duty is good with money and trustworthy. Your eight-year-old is probably not the best bet.

This aspect of the book table should move quickly and efficiently.

One last aside to consider is that for the purpose of your launch, you may want to discount the cost of your book from its standard RRP to make it more enticing to guests.

Additional needs
for the launch

All your launch really needs is yourself, your book, a locale, and your guests. But here are some other things you might consider.

A podium
From which you and your launcher will talk. It's not essential, but a podium naturally screams, *Look at me!*

A microphone
So you can be heard over your guests. Useful if you have lots of people or are softly spoken.

Promotional paraphernalia
You might have the cover of your book blown up and printed into a

poster. If your book has artwork, you might do the same with that. Or create a bookmark with details of the book and yourself.

Decorations

Not strictly necessary, but you could decorate your venue to suit the theme of your book.

Float

Sounds simple, huh? Unless you're having your launch at a bookstore, you'll have to be responsible for the sale of the book. Make sure you bring plenty of change.

Eftpos

Lots of people don't bring ready cash, but are willing to spend on plastic. If you have a portable eftpos machine, this can be an invaluable tool. Consult your bank about how to set up a debit account.

A speech

Yes, that's right. At a certain point, you're going to be required to talk about yourself and your book. So know what you're going to say. Don't rely on yourself just to wing it.

An extract from your book

This is almost a necessity. Your guests have come to celebrate the launch of your book. It's only right they hear a little bit from it – a little bit which *you* read.

Choose about five minutes worth of reading – which is about five hundred words. You may want to choose less or more. Just remember your audience and consider how an extract from your book will go across.

For instance, two thousand words from the middle of a book eighty thousand words long mightn't make sense without everything that's meant to come before it. Choose something that can stand self-contained.

You could preface your extract with an explanation to offer some context, but it's best if the extract can stand alone, just like a short story or article would.

Most of all, you just want to give your guests a taste of your book – not the whole story! This will tease them and make them want to read the rest.

Tips for public presenting

Many people are nervous about reading in public. If you fall into this category, here are some tips.

Rehearse

Yes, incredibly basic, but rehearse in front of a mirror. Make sure you have the flow of words. A passage that looks great on the page might be a tongue twister when read aloud.

Hold something heavy in your hands

If you shake in public, this might become grossly evident when holding your speech in your trembling hands. Carry something heavy, like a clipboard behind it, to weigh down your hands.

Alcohol and presentation

It might seem like a good idea to down a few wines before you go, but alcohol can make you fumble, cause you to slur, or encourage you to be garrulous. Don't overdo it.

Stand behind your podium

At the very least, remain fixed behind your podium. A lot of people who are inexperienced presenting or uncomfortable reading in public tend to pace. Having a podium or microphone to stand behind can help you keep your position fixed.

Setting up your launch

There's no definitive feng shui for a launch. Much will depend on *where* you're holding your launch and how to best employ the space you're using.

Also consider acoustics and how your voice will play from any one area, as well as lighting.

With all that being said, you may want to consider certain staples.

It's up to you how you arrange them.

A focus centre
Where will the audience be concentrated?

Bookstores might have stages you can use. A library might not, and you'll be left to set-up a chair in the corner, or a podium if you have one available.

The choice is yours.

Just be certain that wherever you set up, the whole room can see and hear you and you will, at all times, remain the focus of attention.

Chairs

Arrange rows of chairs spread concentrically from this point. Allow space for an aisle.

The alternative is to have everybody standing and to have chairs for just the infirm.

A book table

Meaning a table just for your books! Think of displays you see in libraries and in bookstores. Now you have one dedicated just to your book!

This can be placed anywhere, but is best placed in some proximity to the entrance.

That way, your book is the first thing people see when they enter, and it's the last thing they'll see before they leave – useful if they haven't bought it yet!

A food and drinks table

Self-explanatory! But perhaps best not placed too close to the book table, as you don't want a congestion of hungry or thirsty people keeping others away from your book table or spilling wine all over your nice new books.

What happens at the launch

You need to compartmentalise how your launch unfolds. There's no hard and fast rules about what should or shouldn't happen and the precise order. But here's a rough running order of things to consider:

+ Starting time: this is the time specified on your invitations that the launch will begin. You need to allow for stragglers and give guests a bit of time to mingle, so you might wait 15–30 minutes from this time before you begin in earnest.

+ You begin, or the emcee begins, proceedings. The guests are thanked for coming. There might be a little talk about the book or the author. The launcher is introduced.

✦ The launcher talks about you and the book. The launcher might even read an excerpt from the book. The launcher announces the book 'launched' and introduces you.

✦ You go up and talk a little about yourself and the book.

You might talk about how you came up with the idea for your book, the writing process, the people who helped you with it (e.g. friends, editor, agent, publisher, dog, me), and read a little extract from it.

+ Take plenty of pictures of the event, either for your own posterity, or to promote the event (and yourself, and your book) afterwards.

+ Once you're done, retreat to the book table ...

The book table

This is important enough that it deserves a section all of its own.

What happens at the book table?
If you're holding your launch at a bookstore, chances are that guests will have to buy your book from the cashier, just as would occur buying any book in a bookstore.

If you're holding your launch elsewhere, you'll probably have to sell your book directly from the book table.

If this is the case, it'd be great if you can have somebody else responsible for the sale of the book.

You have more important things to deal with. 'What?' you may ask.

Your duty at this point is to sign books. Yes, you!

People will want your signature – and perhaps even a little message – scrawled across your book, so you best get practising.

Recapping

Feeling a bit overwhelmed?

Don't be. Let's go over all the steps:

+ Choose a launch date

+ Find somebody to launch your book

+ Schedule a launch venue

+ Send out invitations

+ Advertise your launch

+ Set-up your launch with a focus centre, a snack table, and a book table

+ Your launch commences and your guests mingle

+ Either you thank, or the emcee thanks, the guests for attending and the launcher is introduced

+ The launcher talks about you, your book, may even read an extract, and introduces you

+ You talk about yourself, your book, read an extract, and thank people for attending

+ You retreat to your book table

+ Guests buy the book from the cashier or from the book table and ask you to sign their book.

Once all that's done and the guests are gone, all that's left is the one thing all the best-selling authors don't tell you about: cleaning-up!

It's a wrap!

These rules aren't rigid. There's flexibility in each step. But they offer a framework on how you can structure your launch.

You are limited only by your imagination ... oh, and by your budget. But even on a shoestring budget you can still arrange a fun and fulfilling launch.

Surely you've arranged some sort of party in your life – at the very least, a birthday. Arranging a launch isn't much different.

Have fun with it.

And good luck!

Busybird Publishing is a small, boutique publisher based in the heart of Montmorency, Victoria.

We produce our own range of books, as well as help authors get their stories out into the world.

Title: *The Book Book*

Price: $18.00

Publication Date: 7 February 2014

Format: Paperback (181x111mm, 148 pages)

ISBN: 978 0 992 4325 0 8

Category: Nonfiction

Everyone has a book in them. We all have a story we want to share with the world. But where do we start?

  The Book Book will help break the process into small, manageable steps, providing invaluable tips, insider knowledge into the publishing industry, as well as the inspiration to get started and to keep writing to the end.

  Don't let this opportunity go to waste!

  Trust in *The Book Book* to help you find the way.

  The Book Book is the very first in our *Easy Publishing Series*. Each book is designed to provide the reader with an easy guide into some aspect of writing and/or publishing.

  The *Easy Publishing Series* is perfect for anybody with an interest in writing, or who's a writer and wondering where to go next.

  Look out for more titles soon!

SELF MADE

Real Australian Business Stories

8 Aussie small businesses share their secrets for long-term success

Title: *Self Made: Real Australian Business Stories*

Price: $18.00

Publication Date: 14 February 2014

Format: Paperback (111x181mm, 143 pages)

ISBN: 978 0 9924874 3 0

Category: Nonfiction

The biggest threat in business is ignorance. So many people buy businesses, not completely aware of the responsibilities and demands they'll be undertaking. They make mistakes that cost them time, money, and peace of mind, and hurt their businesses.

Self-Made: Real Australian Business Stories contains eight biopics from business owners who've been there and done that – they've made their mistakes, picked themselves up, learned the hard way, and are now successes in their fields.

If you're looking to get into business, or own a business and need hints and tips about how to streamline operations, kickstart productivity, or just find a way to do things better, you can't go past *Self-Made: Real Australian Business Stories*.

Don't delay! Join the ranks of those who are self-made!

Title: *Below the Belt: Experiences with Prostate Cancer*

Price: $25.00

Publication Date: 21 February 2015

Format: Paperback (153x234mm, 205 pages)

ISBN: 978 0 992 5547 3 6

Category: Nonfiction

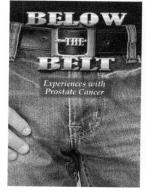

Title: *Journey: Experiences with Breast Cancer*

Price: $32.00

Publication Date: 20 February 2012

Format: Paperback (150x230mm, 326 pages)

ISBN: 978 0 987 1538 0 7

Category: Nonfiction

Our anthologies on cancer – real people sharing their experiences about what they went through, stories that are honest, heartfelt, and raw.

There's a strength which comes from sharing. In reaching out and touching others, we build communities of knowledge and assurance, we let each other know that we are not alone.

A portion of proceeds from *Journey* will go to BreaCan and *WHOW* (Women Helping Other Women), while $5.00 from every *Below the Belt* sold will go to the Prostate Cancer Foundation.

Title: *[untitled]*

Price: Issue 6 ~ $18.00
Issues 3-5 ~ $15.00
Issues 1-2 ~ $10.00

Format: Paperback
(111x180mm)

ISSN: 1836 9065

Category: Fiction Anthology

Title: *page seventeen*

Price: Issues 9-11 ~ $20.00
Issue 8 ~ $15.00
Issue 4 ~ $5.00

Format: Paperback
Issue 11 ~ (176 x 250mm)
Issues 1-10 ~ (148 x 209mm)

ISSN: 1832 5416

Category: Anthology

Our annual anthologies, promoting new and emerging authors from all across the country.

[untitled] is a fantastic collection of just short stories, whereas *page seventeen* includes fiction, poetry, nonfiction, and a cover image competition, the winner's image being used for the cover.

If you would like to submit to either, check our website for details.

Title: *Walk With Me*

Price: $59.95

Publication Date: 22 November 2014

Format: Hardcover (300x300mm, 106 pages)

ISBN: 978 0 9925547 2 9

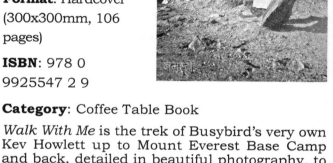

Category: Coffee Table Book

Walk With Me is the trek of Busybird's very own Kev Howlett up to Mount Everest Base Camp and back, detailed in beautiful photography, to raise awareness of Charcot-Marie-Tooth (CMT) disease and funds for the CMT Association Australia.

CMT is an incurable progressive nerve deterioration suffered by 1 in 2,500 people, and a condition also suffered by Kev's own son Dylan. A champion footballer as a teenager, Dylan has had to have both feet reconstructed surgically as a stopgap measure to counter the clawing caused by CMT.

Walk With Me is the journey Kev would've liked to take with Dylan. A photographer with over twenty-five years experience in the commercial photography industry, Kev details his expedition so that you, too, can walk with him to Everest Base Camp and back and not only enjoy the beauty of Nepal, but also contribute to a good cause.

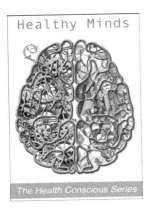
Healthy Minds

The Health Conscious Series

Title: *Healthy Minds*

Price: $25.00

Publication Date: 23 October 2015

Format: Paperback (135x210mm, 182 pages)

ISBN: 978 1 925260 78 8

Category: Nonfiction

The demand for information in the health sector is growing exponentially.

This means that the market for books dealing with health issues is also growing.

Busybird Publishing is proud to be working on a series entitled *HealthConscious*, with each book in the series intending to explore a different aspect of health – from the obvious physical and psychological standpoints, to an exploration of cultural and environmental contributors and their impact on our everyday lives.

Healthy Minds is the first book – an anthology that will contain articles from twelve non-competing professionals, each using their specific expertise to approach the challenge of creating and maintaining a healthy mind.

The importance of this book is demonstrated by the fact that Australian comedian and television presenter Tim Ferguson has agreed to write the foreword. Tim, as you may be aware, has recently disclosed that he suffers from MS.

Healthy Minds is coming soon and will be released as a print book as well as an ebook and distributed worldwide.

Title: *The Writer's Companion 2015-16*

Price: S O L D   O U T !

Publication Date: 18 November 2015

Format: Paperback 210x148mm, 266 pages)

ISBN: 9780992572839

Category: Nonfiction

You want to be a writer, but don't know where to start.

Or you are a writer, and don't know where to submit. The internet's a confusing place, and resources seem limited.

Until now.

The Writer's Companion 2015-16 is an eighteen-month diary, and a brilliant resource for any writer, regardless of your age, level of experience, or intention.

Filled with all sorts of submission opportunities (for publishers, journals, and competitions), *The Writer's Companion 2015-16* will be your everday guide as to where you can send your writing, or give you deadlines to force you to finish that piece that's been nagging you for a while now.

For the writer looking for inspiration, *The Writer's Companion 2015-16* also contains writing prompts and exercises – a perfect way to keep your mind sharp and imagination challenged.

If you're a writer, and have wondered where to turn for help, you can stop looking.

The Writer's Companion 2015-16 is for you.

Note: A new Writer's Companion is released yearly!

Printed in Australia
AUHW020527140622
364914AU00028B/63

9 780992 522605